Into His Hands I Commit

Experiences of a Convert of the Church
of Jesus Christ of Latter-day Saints

Brian Heuett

NEWMAN SPRINGS PUBLISHING
320 Broad Street
Red Bank, NJ 07701

First originally published by Newman Springs Publishing 2021

ISBN 978-1-63881-766-6 (Paperback)
ISBN 978-1-63881-767-3 (Digital)

Printed in the United States of America

To Jody

Contents

Foreword

Brian Heuett is a seeker!

When I first met Brian, I could feel his intense desire to add something more to his life. At this time, he had a nice family, a kind and dedicated mother, a hardworking and very likable father, and three siblings. He was an accomplished athlete, had lots of friends, and was successful in other areas of his life. But there it was—this energized, enthusiastic desire to bring something more into his life. And he did! Which is his story to tell as he does in this book.

From that first encounter, I watched Brian grow and develop in significant ways. I saw Brian several years later in action as a faculty advisor to a university DEX Club student group attending a local competition (a career development event where business students compete to test their knowledge in sales, marketing, and other business-related skills). The team had qualified for the state-level competition and now had to travel to participate.

Brian had been instrumental in their training and preparation for this event, and his actions all spoke to what a hands-on and caring mentor he was. He not only cared about them doing their best in the competition, but he also cared about their well-being and comfort. In addition to finding them a comfortable place to stay to meet their physical needs, he also attended to their emotional needs with his nurturing and kind presence, saying, "You can do this!" and other encouragement. Under his leadership and guidance, the team was very successful, earning medals for their work. Many of them advanced on to nationals. Brian made a difference in their young lives.

Brian has a ready smile and a quick gentle laugh. He never laughs at you but with you! He innately knows when to give comic relief to a moment or situation that may get hard. He gives a genuine smile and maybe even a pat on the back. His sense of humor and caring ways always make him pleasant to be around. You cannot miss his sincere gratitude. He is quick and generous with his thank-you! He has an element of solid faith, and he has discovered something sacred to him—gospel truths. He wanted to make them actualities in his life and see what would happen.

Later in life, when I attended the sacrament meeting for his returning missionary son Kyle, I was again afforded a window on the depth of Brian's growth and accomplishments. As the assigned high councilman speaker of the meeting, Brian delivered a most inspirational gospel doctrine and truth-centered talk. It was evidence of the gospel scholar he had become. He closed with a sincere testimony that radiated his love of the Savior and His teachings.

It was palpable how those in attendance felt. There was a heavenly peace. His son finished the meeting speaking as a stalwart son of God who had indeed been a humble, dedicated young missionary. He gave an inspiring report of his two years of service. For me, however, the crowning glory of that day came after the meeting with Brian's parents in the parking lot. I could feel their true joy and righteous pride in the strong good men their son and grandson were. It was truly a time of basking in the peace the Savior promised, and the scriptural phrase "Men are that they might have joy" (2 Nephi 2:25). There was peace and joy that day!

Brian had put in the work! He had brought love, peace, and joy into many lives. He has fostered learning with his students in the classroom. It was a blessing to be his friend through the years. Though there have been ups and downs and hard challenges in his life, Brian has kept a positive perspective. He radiates his love for what is most dear to him—his confidence in the gospel plan. He wants to make things better, give service, and try to help others along the path of earthly life. Brian's zeal in his youth in seeking his own individual spirituality laid a foundation for him to be a helpful servant in God's work.

The writing and publication of this book of his experiences represents his love for his own life and the lives of others. His hope is that readers will be strengthened spiritually and that his experiences will influence their testimonies for good.

Jan Bishop Holiday

Preface

In this book, I have written what I have come to believe are the most important experiences that have made me partly who I have become spiritually over many years. Life has been exciting, meaningful, and gratifying personally, penetrating my heart deeply in many aspects.

Within my heart and mind rings the phrase that Jesus uttered on the cross at the end of His mission when He said, "And when Jesus had cried with a loud voice, he said, Father, into thy hands I commend my spirit: and having said thus, he gave up the ghost" (Luke 23: 46).

Since becoming a member of the Church of Jesus Christ of Latter-day Saints in July of 1981, it has been a goal of mine to try to represent my Savior in all that I do, say, and think—in other words, become more like Christ.

I do not necessarily expect readers to pattern their individual life after my personal experiences in this book. However, if my experiences can inspire, motivate, bring a reader closer to Jesus Christ, and find significant and rewarding spiritual growth reading, this book will have been well worth it.

The following chapters come from experiences I had while growing up and later learning about the Church of Jesus Christ of Latter-day Saints. Each chapter represents a specific part of my life as it unfolded. The chapters are in chronological order of how the experiences happened. This book of experiences is intended to be messages of hope to the reader. There are so many individuals struggling with life's decisions, their testimony, where to turn for help and understanding, and seeking a religion in general.

It is my hope and desire that those who read this book will have an increase in spirit, faith, hope, and charity, including a willingness to repent and come unto Jesus Christ and be converted unto Him. In other words, accept the invitation to come "Into His Hands" and be blessed in abundance. My desire would be that the same encouragement I experienced both temporally and spiritually from the experiences written on the following pages will be the same encouragement to those who are struggling or seeking eternal truths. May the reader know it is my intent to "succor the weak, lift up the hands which hang down, and strengthen the feeble knees" (Doctrine and Covenants 81:5).

I am grateful to many who have contributed to this work: to the saints of the Spokane Eight Ward and Spokane East Stake for the opportunities of service in various capacities to help me grow personally both spiritually and temporally; Newman Springs Publishing for the insights and helpful suggestions both in thought and style; to my dear friend Jan Bishop Holiday for her encouragement to write, for helpful suggestions on thought, and for the foreword; especially Jody Lynn Heuett for her encouragement and patience to allow me to write the book and being there every step of the way with me.

Brian Laine Heuett
Cedar City, Utah

Personal Life

Hi, my name is Brian Laine Heuett. I was born on April 14, 1960, in Spokane, Washington, to Max and Sheryl Heuett. I am the oldest of four children in the family, consisting of two younger brothers and one sister.

I attended Beamis Elementary School from kindergarten through third grade. It was an older school at the time. However, that did not take away from the wonderful experiences I had with classmates and teachers I had. I vividly remember that the playground was very large in size and had numerous playground equipment for the kids to play on. It was on that playground I first began to learn how to throw a football, play catch with a baseball, and shoot a basketball on a short rim. At that age, it was ball tag I enjoyed the most.

During the summer after my third-grade year, my family sold our home on Smith Street and moved to the Spokane Valley to a community called Greenacres. My parents bought a five-acre farm. The unique part of this home and property was that it was located very close to the I-90 freeway. We lived on Cataldo Street, which was the frontage road to the freeway. It took some time to get used to the loud trucks and cars traveling on the freeway, especially at night when trying to go to sleep.

When school started in the fall, I attended Greenacres Elementary School. It was my fourth-grade year, and I instantly made friends and felt very comfortable attending school at Greenacres. It was during my fifth- and sixth-grade years that school really became enjoyable for me personally. I had great teachers, and I played on the school basketball and baseball teams. It was during this time I made many lifelong friendships and learned to develop my skills and love of sports. And I was a pretty good marble player on the playground.

In fall of 1973, I attended Greenacres Junior High School. It was my seventh-grade year. Many of my classmates from grade school were attending the junior high with me, and I made new friends from several other grade schools in the district that were attending Greenacres Junior High. The mascot of the school was the bruins, which suited me fine because the UCLA Bruins were my favorite college basketball team at the time.

I participated on the football, basketball, and baseball teams that year, truly enjoying sports in a competitive manner and further developing my personal skills on each of the sports. I played defensive end and backup quarterback on the football team, small forward and guard on the basketball team, and first base and pitched on the baseball team.

The seventh grade was a successful year, and I give much of the credit to the wonderful teachers and friends I had throughout the year.

The following year my eighth-grade year was considerably more challenging academically. The classes were in-depth, and the teachers were tougher in their grading. Or it was my lack of learning the material. I continued to play football, basketball, and baseball on the school teams. I enjoyed the school environment for the social, academic, and personal growth that came with being a student. I really enjoyed my history courses and some of the science courses I was enrolled in throughout the year. I didn't enjoy English writing, except for the reading part of the course; I enjoyed reading books. I had no interest in the math courses, never thought I needed to learn it if I wasn't going to use the principles of math in life later.

In fall of 1976, I entered the ninth grade. It was a year of school I would never forget. Academically, all my courses were interesting and enjoyable. Some of my best friends at the time were in the same classes, and the teachers were outstanding. I participated in all three sports, and as an individual and team, we were very competitive and always in the top spot in the standings or right near the top. Our coaches were the best, had our best interest at heart, and knew how to coach us both individually and collectively.

During the ninth grade, I recognized that some of my friends whom I came to respect, admire, and enjoy being around were different in the way they lived life and the characteristics that made them who they were. Learning about them and their personal life, I learned they belonged to the Church of Jesus Christ of Latter-day Saints. Not knowing much about this religion, I began asking questions and finding out details of what these friends believed and worshipped. It became clear to me these friends were unique and peculiar. My respect and admiration became a conviction in my heart for who they were as individuals.

Overall, my junior high school days were memorable and well worth all that I experienced.

From 1977 to 1979, I attended Central Valley High School. Our school mascot were the bears. School colors were blue and white. As a class, we became very close in our friendships and took the time to get to know everyone in our class.

It was during my sophomore year that I didn't participate in football so I could focus on basketball and baseball. Once high school began, two junior high schools came together in high school. Greenacres and Evergreen junior high made up our high school class. Both junior high schools had tremendous athletic talent, and it made for a very competitive team in high school. The basketball team and baseball team were outstanding and won many games compared to few losses.

The year I will remember the most of my school experiences will be my senior year, 1979, at Central Valley High School. There were very few classmates that I didn't know, and most of them were dear friends of mine regardless of the walk of life they were experiencing.

Academically, I had done well in high school, and my teachers were phenomenal. I enjoyed learning and gaining life experiences and lessons that would set the stage for the rest of my life.

Athletically, our basketball team made the Greater Spokane League District tournament where we were eliminated in the second game. The baseball team had a tremendous year battling for the league championship right up to the last game of the regular season. We were eliminated in the district tournament, and with that came a heavy and torn heart that would sting for months to come. There were several players on that team that year that went on to play college baseball, and one signed a professional contract. It was an experience I was involved with that I will never forget.

In addition to school and sports, I had summer jobs working for the school district changing sprinkler pipes, working with my dad hauling hay, taking care of farm animals, and roofing houses. Some of my favorite things to do was riding horses, antagonizing the pigs until they were in hysterics or my mom caught me. My brother Dale and I would feed the cattle in a trough and go around on the opposite side, grab the cow's horns, and determine who could hold on the longest. We had a hay day, no pun intended, doing this sometimes for an hour.

We took family vacations during the summer. Most memorable was the trip we took to Banff, Canada. Such beautiful country and a peaceful, serene experience. We had a memorable trip to Yellowstone National Park. What was memorable was sitting on the side of I-90 for several hours, waiting for help after blowing the water pump in the car. After being towed back to the nearest town and spending the night in the parking lot in the tent trailer, we were helped the next day. After nearly an all-day mechanical job putting in a new water pump, we were on our way. It was exhausting for all of us. But we made it to Yellowstone and spent the next few days touring the park.

A couple of hilarious moments while in the park. My dad stopped near some elk alongside the road. My brother Dale, the daring one, got out of the car to take a close-up picture. He got too close, and one of the elk charged him while stomping its front hooves into the ground. That was the fastest I ever seen the kid move.

The next day, we were moving along with the traffic. It was late afternoon or early evening when people spotted a moose in a meadow. We pulled over and got out of the car and were standing with other people. I heard someone in the crowd say, "Where is that guy going?" I looked up, and my dad had made his way out into the meadow quite a way when someone yelled, "It's charging!"

I looked, and the moose was trotting toward my dad. I thought like father, like son, when it comes to common sense of wild animals. My dad started to retreat toward the highway, and the moose gave up the chase. My mom, in her quiet tone of voice, read him his rights; and that was the last time anyone got out of the car to take pictures or get a closer look. In the long run, it made for good discussion over the next several years.

The following two summer's after graduation, I was privileged to play semi-pro baseball with a local team in Spokane, WA. It, too, was an experience that brought great excitement to me personally. It was during this time of April 1981, that I had an experience that would change my life forever.

The following chapters describe in detail the experiences that would bring more meaning to my life than anything I had experienced at that time.

The Invitation

Ask, and it shall be given you; Seek and ye shall
find; Knock, and it shall be opened unto you.

—Matthew 7:7

It was mid-April of 1981, when I was invited to the home of the
Skougen family whom I knew quite well for dinner. Arriving at their
home around five in the afternoon, I was invited into the home and
asked to sit on the couch and make myself comfortable. Shortly
after I arrived, the doorbell rang, and two young men entered the
home. Both were wearing white shirts, ties, slacks, nice shoes and
had a smile from ear to ear. I had noticed similar young men around
the community riding bikes or walking along the road. I stood and
shook hands with each one of them as we were introduced. I was told
to relax and that the elders were not there to preach to me the word
of God or convert me to some religion. At least not yet!

After final preparations were made with the dinner, we were
all asked to sit around the table. Those present were family, friends,
and two elders serving missions for the Church of Jesus Christ of
Latter-day Saints. The conversation focused on where the elders grew
up and a little of their individual background. I was asked to share
some of my background and life, which I was a little reluctant at first.
However, engaging in the visit, I shared a few thoughts.

After dinner, the missionaries (elders) left for another engage-
ment they had scheduled that evening. After the table was cleared off
and the kitchen was clean, I retired to the living room where more

visiting took place. After a few minutes, Brother Skougen asked me a big question that I was not anticipating now. I was asked, if I ever considered learning about the "Mormon" church, better known as the Church of Jesus Christ of Latter-day Saints.

My response was, I could not give an answer at that time but would think about it. Feeling the family was content with my response, the discussion moved to other topics the rest of the evening. After another hour passed, and I felt my welcome had come to an end for the evening. I gave my thanks for a wonderful evening and said my goodbyes.

On my way home that evening, I was consumed in my thoughts with the question that was asked of me. "Would you ever consider learning about the Church of Jesus Christ of Latter-day Saints?" The impressions were very strong and real, more real than anything else I had ever felt in my life at that point.

I thought of the kindness from the missionaries and the special feeling I had while in their presence. As I turned down the street, I lived on and drove the last short distance to my home. After getting inside, I called my dear friend that night and told him I would be willing to meet again with the missionaries and his family. However, I was not to be pressured or asked to make any promises I did not feel comfortable with. He told me that he would make sure the missionaries would not pressure me or ask me to commit to anything dealing with conversion, believing doctrine I didn't understand.

Missionary Discussions

Learn of me, and listen to my words; walk in meekness
of my Spirit; and you shall have peace in me.

—Doctrine and Covenants 19:9

The following week, I met with the Skougen family and the elders. I
was taught the steps to prayer and how I should address my Heavenly
Father. The sequence was taught in this order: First, address God as
your Heavenly Father; second, give Him thanks for all the things you
are most grateful for; third, ask Him for the things you stand in need
of; and fourth, close the prayer in the Name of Jesus Christ.

After that quick lesson, I was asked to offer the opening prayer.
Before doing so, I mentioned I was being set up by the elders. There
was a chuckle by all that were present. I offered what seemed like an
awkward prayer which was very stressful for me personally. One of
the elders said I passed on my very first try.

We continued to the next lesson, which consisted of the Plan of
Salvation and the purpose of life. I received some pamphlets to read
along with a copy of the Book of Mormon. This lesson, we discussed
life before earth life and how we all lived as individual spirits in the
premortal life with God and Jesus Christ. We did not have bodies
of flesh and bones like we do here as mortal beings on earth. We
learned in the premortal life and were part of what was called the war
in heaven, where we voted for one of two plans—Jesus Christ's plan
or Lucifer's plan.

This lesson resonated with me in a very deep-seated spiritual way. It made perfect sense to me!

I drove home that night with a different sense of the spirit, most likely not recognizing what it was tugging at my heart.

The second week, things progressed, and the lesson consisted of learning about the Book of Mormon. Part of the lesson this week consisted of reading scriptures from the Book of Mormon and learning the proper interpretation and the meaning of the passages presented. As the lesson advanced, it became clear to me that I was holding and reading from a very special book that was translated by the prophet Joseph Smith Jr. and that it was different from the Bible in some respects.

Though different, the Book of Mormon had a powerful spirit about its pages that drew me closer to its words, desiring to know more. The elders asked me if I would kneel in prayer at some time soon and ask my Heavenly Father if the Book of Mormon was true. With excitement in my voice, I said it would be a privilege to find out for myself if the Book of Mormon was the word of prophets and the life of Jesus Christ.

The next several weeks, the elders continued teaching me the eternal principles of the gospel of the Church of Jesus Christ of Latter-day Saints. We began meeting at my home where I lived on my own at the time. I continued working, coaching Little League baseball, and playing in a semipro baseball league. During this time, I spent much of my time reading the Book of Mormon daily, usually during my lunch break and in the evening after returning home at the end of the day.

During this period in my life, something was happening to me, mostly spiritually. I could feel it in my heart, and I recognized that my thoughts were focused on a God that I always believed was there but wasn't sure how to know for sure. I frequently went to my knees in deep, sincere, heartfelt prayer. At first, it felt a little awkward, but as I continued praying several times a day, it became more comfortable and I found strength in praying.

Reading the Book of Mormon was very interesting, and it intrigued me in many ways. I realized it was part of history that I had never learned before, but it resonated with me in a very real sense. The longer I read, the harder it was to put the book down. When I would read, I noticed I was happier and enthusiastic about life in general. My days seemed to be filled with joy, and it seemed I was successful in the things I was pursuing in life at that time.

I truly enjoyed spending preparation day with the missionaries, playing basketball and watching church history videos. They would come to my home almost daily and teach me more about the gospel or leave an inspirational thought.

In the month of June 1981, I set a goal that I would make a significant effort through prayer to find out whether or not the Book of Mormon was true or not. It was a Saturday. I was home relaxing when I had an urge to go to my bedroom, kneel in prayer, and ask my Heavenly Father if the gospel was true and if the Book of Mormon truly was the word of God.

I knelt with sincerity, humility, and confidence, having no fears to know the truth about the principles I had been taught or the words I had read in the Book of Mormon. On that given Saturday morning, after asking God if the religious principles I had been taught by friends and the missionaries were truly things I should accept into my life at that time and were those principles, a very short and quick response penetrated my soul.

With vividness and all the tender feelings of my heart, I came to know for a surety that the gospel of the Church of Jesus Christ of Latter-day Saints was the eternal truth on the earth. Having no doubts, nothing wavering, I had come to know the truth of what I had been wanting to know for several weeks. As I raised up off my knees, my eyes were moist with tears and I felt as though my strength had been taken from me. I realized I had been given the opportunity to come to know the reality and power of prayer when performed with genuine, heartfelt desires.

A Change of Heart

And now behold, I ask of you, my brethren of the
church, have ye Spiritually been born of God? Have
ye received his image in your countenances? Have ye
experienced this mighty change in your hearts?

—Alma 5:14

On one of the elder's preparation day, they had an appointment to attend to. While they were gone, I stayed in their apartment and watched the video of the First Vision. Before watching the video, I prayed that I might come to know if Joseph Smith Jr. indeed was a living prophet, restored the gospel of Jesus Christ back on the earth in its fullness, and if he truly had a vision of God the Father and His Son Jesus Christ.

There was a spirit present during the video, and I would feel emotional. I found myself having a great respect for Joseph Smith Jr. to have the courage to go and find out the answer to his prayers. When young Joseph left the grove, he uttered, "For I had seen a vision; I knew it, and I knew God knew it, and I could not deny it, neither dared I do it; at least I knew that by so doing I would offend God, and come under condemnation" (Joseph Smith—History 1:25).

When I heard this phrase in the video and read the passage in the Joseph Smith—History portion of scripture, nothing became clearer to my ears and penetrated my heart with such belief as did these words uttered by the young Joseph Smith Jr.

I knew at that moment the vision Joseph Smith Jr. said he had was true. I realized that God did have living prophets on the earth and that He communicated His will through these prophets to His children. I knew that Joseph Smith Jr. truly saw God the Father and His Son Jesus Christ and received counsel from them in preparing to restore the gospel in all its ordinances, teachings, and priesthood to prepare for the second coming of Christ to the earth.

This experience sealed my conviction of living prophets on earth, and "I committed myself in His hands."

Time was quickly passing by, and much had been taught with regard to the gospel principles in a short time. It made sense to me, and I was able to connect personally and spiritually with what I was hearing and reading. On several occasions, it resonated with me that there was a change taking place within my soul. My heart had and continued to change as I made God and Jesus Christ a greater part of my life. Things that had bothered me before didn't seem to have an effect on me. I was able to forgive people who had communicated sarcastic, hurtful, and painstaking comments to me about attending the Church of Jesus Christ of Latter-day Saints.

If there was one characteristic that I noticed more than anything else during this time, it was that I focused on the true happiness in general that occurred in my life. While reading the scriptures or offering up my personal prayers, I felt closer to my Savior and really grasped the idea and feeling that my heart was going through a sanctification process. It was an amazing experience and one that I could not control necessarily.

Overall, for the first time in my life, it was apparent that the things that mattered most had revealed itself to me, especially spiritually. And in doing so, it was apparent that my heart had gone through a mighty change, impacting my mind and spirit both spiritually and temporally.

It was a time of great excitement for me, and a new and everlasting religious sect was unfolding right before my eyes. There was no way to slow it down, nor did I want it to slow down. I knew in my heart that I had crossed paths with a religion that would edify me immensely when times of troubled waters surrounded me, and they would from time to time.

Consent

And all things shall be done by common consent
in the church, by much prayer and faith, for all
things you shall receive by faith. Amen.

—Doctrine and Covenants 26:2

On Sunday, the day after coming to know the truth of my prayers and after church, I invited the elders to my home, saying that I would like to visit with them. The elders knocked on my door, and I let them in. After greeting them and thanking them for coming over, I asked them to please have a seat. I had something I needed to tell them.

We talked about church and our meetings we attended during church. I asked them if they had appointments with other individuals the rest of the day. Elder Hansen asked me, "What do you want to share with us?"

I told him that I didn't want him to be mad at me. He and I with his companions had spent several hours together, and they had done so much for me the last several months. I began to reveal to them in a very sad and low tone of voice that I appreciated all they had done and the wonderful friends they had become to me. It was very apparent by the looks on their face that they felt and knew that I was going to ask that they not come by anymore.

Watching their shoulders slump lower and lower and their heads hang low, it became clear to me they could bear no more and had reached the moment of greatest despair and sick feeling one might encounter. I sprang to my feet and communicated to them that I wanted to be baptized. Elder Hansen, who had become my best friend at the time, was so shocked at my behavior and fell off the footstool he was sitting on, landing on his back on the floor. All he could do was holler and scream that he was going to hurt me real bad for playing such a horrible joke on them.

I cried with joy and laughed with pity for those two poor elders. It was a Sunday of spiritual growth where the heavens had opened, and pure, genuine revelation had been received. It was a day of joy and happiness for so many that had worked so faithfully for this great experience to come to pass. After much prayer, reading, teaching, hard work, and patience, the Lord had blessed my life in great abundance.

You can imagine the rest of the day I spent answering my phone. Others came by my home, and I spent significant time repenting for what I had done to the elders. It was amazing how quickly the word traveled that I had consented in becoming a member of the Church of Jesus Christ of Latter-day Saints. It was an amazing feeling that I was going to become a part of God's only true and eternal gospel on the earth.

A short time later, my name was announced in sacrament meeting that I had been baptized and confirmed a member of the church, and through common consent, my name was presented to the ward members. It was exciting to see all the hands raise in the air, supporting my membership into the church and ward. My heart felt so much love and excitement at that moment for the wonderful people that were present in the sacrament program that day.

Repentance

And we know that all men must repent and believe on
the name of Jesus Christ, and worship the Father in
his name, and endure in faith on his name to the end,
or they cannot be saved in the kingdom of God.

—Doctrine and Covenants 20:29

On Friday, 17th of July 1981, I was able to meet with the elder who
was holding the position of zone leader and had an interview for baptism. He asked me a sequence of several questions which I answered.
It was a very positive interview and one of more learning. He con-
gratulated me for the choice I made to be baptized and become a
member of the Church of Jesus Christ of Latter-day Saints. He shook
my hand, gave me a hug, and went about our day.

During the evening, the same day, I met with Bishop Scott of
the Spokane Eight Ward. He too asked me a series of questions which
appeared to be in the direction of repentance and forgiveness. At one
point in the interview, the bishop asked me to list all the things in my
life that I would like to have wiped clean from my slate at the time of
baptism. I thought for a few seconds and began to verbally tell him
things I wish I could take back, replace with better choices, repair
feelings in others I had hurt, tried harder in school, read scriptures
in the Bible more often, not attend the St. Luther Church where I
was baptized as a young boy, and things I said that I knew were not
nice or right.

When this interview was over, Bishop Scott shared with me that the next day when I was baptized and came up out of the water, all these things he had listed on the chalkboard would be removed from me and that God will have forgiven me of all the wrongs in my life up to that time. Bishop Scott shared some verses of scripture with me and told me to never forget the principles being taught by the Savior.

> Fear not to do good, my sons, for whatsoever ye sow, that shall ye also reap; therefore, if ye sow good ye shall also reap good for your reward.
>
> Therefore, fear not, little flock; do good; let earth and hell combine against you, for if ye are built upon my rock, they cannot prevail.
>
> Behold, I do not condemn you; go your ways and sin no more; perform with soberness the work which I have commanded you.
>
> Look unto me in every thought; doubt not, fear not.
>
> Behold the wounds which pierced my side, and also the prints of the nails in my side, and also in my hands and feet; be faithful, keep my commandments, and ye shall inherit the kingdom of heaven. Amen. (Doctrine and Covenants 6:33–37)

Bishop Scott shared his testimony with me and then asked me to share my testimony with him. It was a special moment between the two of us. When I was done, the bishop mentioned that I focused on Joseph Smith Jr. and his experience as the significant role of my conversion. I communicated to my bishop that it was probably an accurate assessment.

He told me at that time that it was understandable but that I should remember we worship and look toward God the Father and His Son Jesus Christ, and that is where the center core of the gospel rests. I assured him that I would place my focus and testimony on the shoulders of the trinity of the Godhead from thereon. He asked me to offer a closing prayer. We shook hands and went about our evening.

As I drove home that evening, I thought about what the bishop said and the impact that had on me personally.

Once again, the spirit touched my heart of the love and kindness that my Savior and my Heavenly Father had for me. I realized I was really one of God's children.

Baptism and Confirmation

All those who humble themselves before God and desire to be baptized, and come forth with broken hearts and contrite spirits, and witness before the church that they have truly repented of all their sins, and are willing to take upon them the name of Jesus Christ, having a determination to serve him to the end, and truly manifest by their works that they have received of the Spirit of Christ unto the remission of their sins, shall be received by baptism into the Church.

—Doctrine and Covenants 20:37

Baptism

On July 18, 1981, I arrived at the church building where I was fitted for a baptismal suit. It was an exciting time for me, and I was overcome with emotion and joy at the time. I was able to look in the font and see what it looked like, then changed into my baptismal clothes and came back to the foyer where I engaged with others while people took pictures.

At two in the afternoon in the Evergreen Relief Society room in Veradale, Washington, of the Church of Jesus Christ of Latter-day Saints, the baptism services began. There was a talk on baptism and its covenants by Elder Osbourn. He was a tall, broad-shouldered individual with red hair. I loved his spirit and disposition. He was a good missionary. Afterward, I was escorted to the edge of the baptismal font. I walked down the steps into the warm water followed by Brother Skougen. Brother Skougen took me by the hand, raising his right arm, uttered the baptismal prayer, immersed me in the water, and pulled me back up. Obviously, we were both extremely wet. He gave me a big hug, and we exited the baptismal font.

Confirmation

> And to confirm those who are baptized into the church,
> by the laying on of hands for the baptism of fire and
> the Holy Ghost, according to the scriptures.
>
> —Doctrine and Covenants 20:41

A few minutes later, we reentered the Relief Society room where everyone was waiting for us. There was a talk on the Holy Ghost by Elder Art Hansen. He had become an instrumental part of my conversion and a dear friend to me. We had much in common: sports, the outdoors, family, friends, and now religious beliefs. He was from Boulder, Colorado, and loved to snow ski. I must mention here that the first time I met Elder Hansen at the Skougen family home, there was an instant spiritual connection between Elder Hansen and myself. He had a smile on his face, a genuine personality, very social, and was easy to talk to.

After his talk, I was invited to come to the front of the room and take a seat in a chair that was provided for me. Elder Hansen placed his hands on my head and several other individuals, including Bishop Scott and laid their hands on top of Elder Hansen's hands. Elder Hansen confirmed me a member of the Church of Jesus Christ of Latter-day Saints and said unto me, "Receive the Holy Ghost." He then pronounced a blessing following the promptings of the spirit on me.

The feelings circulating through my soul were indescribable. But I knew they were true and straight from my Heavenly Father to me personally. I felt myself succumbing to the spirit, and it filled me internally like I had never felt before. I recall thinking I am a true disciple of Jesus Christ now. I belonged to His Church and can serve Him, my family, and friends.

It was a day I will remember for many years to come. My heart was full of love and gratification for all of those who played a role on the program and made sure I followed through with my commitment. In attendance were high school classmates that were already members who set wonderful examples for me: the likes of Sister Mott, Andreas, Christiansen, Sister Bishop and her family, and Brother Pendergrass. Several others were there, and I felt so much love from all of these great saints—many who fellowshipped me along the way and played a pivotal role in my parents' conversion later on.

Following the services, several of us went to Dairy Queen for ice cream and celebrated. The day was filled with an edifying spirit and happiness for all who were there.

Once returning home and changing out of my suit and putting on some comfortable and cooler clothes, I went to the living room and sat in my favorite rocking chair in front of the glass window. I closed my eyes and took a deep breath and began to recapture the events that had taken place the last two and a half hours.

At some point, I opened my scriptures to recall and read what had been taught earlier in the day. We learned that "baptism is itself a new and everlasting covenant" (Doctrine and Covenants 22). As mentioned in Mosiah, by being baptized we are "called to be his people, and are willing to bear one another's burdens, that they may be light; are willing to mourn with those that mourn; yea, and comfort those that stand in need of comfort, and to stand as witnesses of God at all times and in all things, and in all places that ye may be in, even until death, that ye may be redeemed of God, and be numbered with those of the first resurrection, that ye may have eternal life" (Mosiah 18:8–9).

Continuing to read in Mosiah, I was reminded that "those who actually enjoy the gift of the Holy Ghost are the ones who are born again, who have become new creatures of the Holy Ghost" (Mosiah 27:24–26).

Realizing I was privileged to be a part of God's team now and having the blessing of remembering and knowing of the scriptures at an early stage of converting to the church was the beginning of something very important to come. I was a blessed man currently.

Aaronic Priesthood

And the lesser priesthood continued, which priesthood holdeth the key of the ministering of angels and the preparatory gospel.

—Doctrine and Covenants 84:26

The following Sunday, July 19, 1981, I was interviewed by Bishop Scott and found worthy to be ordained to the office of a priest in the Aaronic Priesthood by Brother Skougen. Those present were Brother Skougan and the bishopric. There was a special spirit during the ordination, and I could feel the excitement and enthusiasm from those involved in the process.

After the ordination and blessing were completed, the bishop and I visited for about a half hour about the Aaronic Priesthood and the importance of it in my life. He had me open my scriptures to section 20 of the Doctrine and Covenants, and we read together the following: "The priest's duty is to preach, teach, expound, exhort, and baptize, and administer the sacrament, and visit the house of each member, and exhort them to pray vocally and in secret and attend to all family duties. And he may ordain other priests, teachers, and deacons" (Doctrine and Covenants 20:45–48).

The bishop and I broke down each characteristic mentioned in these verses and discussed the meaning and importance of each with regard to the Aaronic Priesthood as a priest. After discussing the duties of a priest, he encouraged me to be a good example to the other priests, teachers, and deacons in the ward to encourage them to make wise decisions and remember who they are by providing uplifting service when possible.

I remember the bishop teaching me that the priesthood is for providing service to our fellow man, help build the kingdom of God, and bring individuals unto Christ.

I was amazed at the privileges that just kept coming. I truly was witnessing miracles in my life in a short time. It wasn't long before I was able to put the priesthood to work after having it bestowed upon me.

Ward fellowshipping

And behold, I tell you these things that ye may learn wisdom;
that ye may learn that when ye are in the service of your
fellow beings ye are only in the service of your God.

—Mosiah 2:17

Shortly after receiving the Aaronic Priesthood, President Packard approached me at church and asked me if I would be willing to house-sit for a sister in the ward that could not be home with her husband who was quite ill. Having the time to spend a few hours a day to help, President Packard introduced me to Brother and Sister Ramsey. A couple of days later, I arrived at the home of the Ramseys, and Sister Ramsey taught me the protocol of what my assignment would consist of.

A list was created of medicines and the times of day Brother Ramsey was to receive them. When he was to have lunch, he was given a choice of foods in the morning. It typically consisted of soup, a sandwich, or leftovers from the night before.

One of Brother Ramsey's favorite parts of the day involved me reading the Book of Mormon to him about half hour before lunch. He would lay in bed while I sat in a chair next to the bed, and he could hear me while reading. Frequently, he would stop me and ask a series of questions about what I had read and give him an explanation. After about two weeks of this routine, I was driving home and pondering a question Brother Ramsey asked me. He had me read a scripture to him: "But learn that he who doeth the works of righteousness shall receive his reward, even peace in this world, and eternal life in the world to come" (Doctrine and Covenants 59:23).

He asked me what I thought that scripture meant. Being a new convert to the church and with a juvenile understanding of the scriptures, I gave him my best answer which consisted of, "By doing good, we will be blessed both on earth and in heaven."

He responded with "Good answer," and encouraged me to continue reading and learning from the scriptures.

Later in the month, building the courage to ask Brother Ramsey why he liked me to read the Book of Mormon to him each day, I asked. His response was both shocking and revealing. Brother Ramsey, with a smile on his face, answered my question by the following statement: "I have read the Book of Mormon more times than I can count. I love it. I cherish it. It is true. My prayers have been answered from reading it. My understanding of Jesus Christ has become sacred. I hear His voice through reading the Book of Mormon.

"I want to leave this life knowing that through you, I was able to read the Book of Mormon one last time, but this time, you can begin the journey I began many years ago by reading the Book of Mormon." He promised if I would read daily, I would find joy and peace my whole life.

The next day, tending to Brother Ramsey's needs and following the routine, he called me into his room and asked me to open his closet door and pull some of his suits out and lay them on the bed. I held each suit up while he shared a short story about an act of service he had while wearing a specific suit. There were four of them!

When he was done sharing his stories, he asked me politely to take the suits home, have them dry-cleaned, and wear them. It was a gift to me for what I had done for him. A few days later, Brother Ramsey peacefully passed away. When the news reached me, my heart was heavy and I wept for all that he had done in my behalf. I was going to miss him. He fellowshipped me in the gospel and taught me some of the important things of life right up to his last day. He was a man of God!

I could list hundreds of names of people who played such a significant role in my growth in the gospel. The people of the Spokane Eight Ward were the epitome of what every ward should be like when fellowshipping a new member of the Church of Jesus Christ of Latter-day Saints. I felt appreciated and accepted in the ward from day one. I was not only invited, but some told me I had to play on the ward softball and basketball teams. I was asked to coach the youth men's team. I referred during the basketball season. I attended as many ward activities and socials as I could. If there was an Elder's Quorum activity—for example, a barbeque—I was invited and went there.

Some of the ward members came to me and asked if I would reach out to their son or daughter who I attended school with and invite them back to church or to activities.

There was one family in the ward, the bishop's, that I became very close to and spent time in their home with their family nearly every Sunday. Later, they became my second family. I was involved with their family home evenings occasionally and attended sporting events of the kids in the family. Sister Bishop and I would talk about the scriptures and how they related to life's challenges. Janet and I talked about the importance of serving a mission, schooling, discussing the scriptures, and stake and general conference talks when it was that time of the year.

I give much of the credit to those saints of the ward at that time for being where I am today. The examples, love, testimonies, and friendship I felt will always be a part of who I became as a convert of the Church of Jesus Christ of Latter-day Saints.

On several occasions, my communication to others has been that it is my prayer that every member of the eight ward will be found worthy to enter the celestial kingdom just for the fellowshipping they provided to me personally. I always prayed the Lord's choicest blessing would be upon their heads twofold. I will be eternally grateful for my fellow brothers and sisters in the Spokane Eight Ward.

First Speaking Assignment

And this is the ensample unto them, that they shall
speak as they are moved upon by the Holy Ghost.

—Doctrine and Covenants 68:3

A few weeks after I was baptized, I was approached by Brother Davenport of the bishopric and asked if I would prepare a talk for the sacrament services. I asked him what the topic would be, and he said, "Repentance." I answered in the affirmative and went home for the rest of the day.

During the week, my anxiety grew and grew about this talk coming on Sunday. I had never delivered a talk before. I didn't know how to research the topic, and I felt completely overwhelmed. Sunday arrived, and I decided to miss church. Without a moment's hesitation, I knew in my heart someone would be visiting me later that day. Sure enough, Brother Davenport came to the house and wanted to visit with me. He asked me why I was not in church. I shared with him what I had been experiencing during the week and could not deliver on this speaking assignment.

Two days later, I found myself in Brother Davenport's home learning how to research my topic on repentance, which seemed more applicable at the time than the week before. I was able to look through past talks, scriptures, and other resources Brother Davenport made available to me. After gathering enough reading material, he coached me how to make an outline and develop my talk for the coming Sunday. I thanked him and headed home.

Over the next few days, I read and highlighted the material I had collected. I put my thoughts on paper in an organized outline and started to review my notes until I felt comfortable with my talk. My confidence grew as I became better prepared and comfortable with the words on paper.

Sunday came. I drove to church and walked into the chapel where a few people had started taking their seats in the pews. I was asked to have a seat on the stand, and the only comfort I found in that was the seat was cushioned and well padded. I had tremendous anxiety and felt sick to my stomach. I tried to breathe slowly and talk to myself like I did during sports.

On the days I was pitching, I would get anxiety during the day, but I found a way to rehearse the game in my mind and visualize being successful and having command of my pitches. I began to rehearse my talk in my mind, looked over my notes, visualized myself standing at the podium, and taking command of my feelings and thoughts.

The sacrament was blessed and passed to the congregation. Afterward, Brother Davenport stood and announced the speaking order for the services. I was the second speaker, and I was hoping the first speaker would talk for about thirty minutes. Instead, the speaker being one of the youths in the ward, took about five minutes. I thought to myself, *I will read my talk quickly and be done and the final speaker will have to fill the remaining time.*

It was my turn to speak, and I stood to deliver my prepared speech. Scared to near silence, I uttered the first few words. Not passing out at that point, I thought this was going well. I continued to press on, and before I knew it, my ten minutes had passed and I was done with my first talk in the church. As I sat down, I remember thinking I hoped to never do that again.

After the sacrament services were over, Brother Cabbage approached me and asked a question of me. He said, "Were you experiencing a *Nephite* behind the podium?"

My reply was, "What do you mean?"

He asked me again, "Were you experiencing a *Nephite* behind the podium?" The third time, he told me to watch my knees. As he knocked his knees together, he asked again, "Were you experiencing a knee fight behind the podium?" We both laughed, and he gave me a big hug and told me he was proud of me.

Several ward members came to me and expressed their gratitude and feelings for me. I felt so much support and fellowship from so many people. Lastly, Brother Davenport caught up to me and said, "Well done and don't ever stand me up again." I think it was because the Sunday I missed, he had to fill in for me and he was the one experiencing a knee fight.

The experience I had that day became what I learned to do throughout most of my life: delivering talks in various callings in the church, as a professor teaching public-speaking courses, and as a professional trainer and consultant throughout the USA and Canada.

I was being groomed for something bigger and better and didn't recognize it at the time. In a conversation later with Brother Perks, he mentioned to me, "Don't ever forget the Lord works in 'mysterious ways.'"

Later in the evening, I was explaining to my mom that I had delivered a talk in church and how frightened I was. She told me to have confidence in myself like I always had in my life and to stay with the basic teachings of my beliefs. I was impressed at that moment that her teachings and words made sense to me.

I was reminded of a scripture that Brother Faber had shared with me. In any situation that you are teaching, speaking, conversing about the gospel, it is important to remember: "'Teach the principles of my gospel,' the Lord commands, which are in the Bible and the Book of Mormon, in the which is the fulness of the gospel... And these shall be their teachings, as they shall be directed by the Spirit. And the Spirit shall be given unto you by the prayer of faith; and if ye receive not the Spirit ye shall not teach" (Doctrine and Covenants 42:12–14).

I treasured these things up in my heart. I had learned from a caring and loving bishopric member who helped me prepare and a loving mother who sealed the learning experience with her own words yet spoken and taught from the heart.

A Teacher

And again, the elders, priests and teachers, of this church shall
teach the principles of my gospel, which are in the Bible and the
Book of Mormon, in the which is the fulness of the gospel.

—Doctrine and Covenants 42:12

Once I committed to the bishop that I would do my very best to live
up to my priesthood responsibilities, he asked me if I would accept
a calling in the ward. Things seemed to be coming so quickly, and I
felt like I was losing my grip on where this was all taking me. After
catching my breath and the shock calmed down, I asked, "What is it
you would like me to do?"

The bishop said, "I would like you to teach the fourteen-year-
old Sunday school course?" I told him I had never taught a class like
that before. He said, "You will do great, and we will have you meet
with our Sunday school president for some quick training." I mentioned that it would be needed.

My name was presented to the congregation that day for sus-
taining. I might have been praying it would be a unanimous oppos-
ing. It was not the outcome to say the least. The following Sunday,
I was teaching a large group of fourteen-year-old youth the gospel.
The Book of Mormon course was the focus that year. After several
weeks of teaching, I adjusted and learned to be effective in the classroom, teaching the youth and learning myself. During this time, it
was drawn to my attention that "Jesus Christ is the Master teacher,"

said President Boyd K. Packer, president of the Quorum of the Twelve Apostles, in *Mine Errand from the Lord.*

Over the next several months, I served in the church with enthusiasm and commitment to the Lord. I attended a teacher development course at Brother Faber's home every Sunday for four months. It was there that I learned the scriptures and how to teach with the spirit. What an awesome and amazing experience that was. The first scripture I was able to learn and recite from memory was "Behold, I say unto you that you let your time be devoted to the studying of the scriptures and preaching" (Doctrine and Covenants 26:1). There were about four or five of us enrolled in the class, and we would have scripture chases at the beginning of the class. I was amazed how quickly I was learning where to find the scriptures in the Bible or Book of Mormon.

As we learned to be effective in our teaching, we learned how to have the spirit with us and how to recognize it when it was present. What an amazing experience. There were times the spirit was so powerful in the class that we all were in tears and felt the sweet serene feeling that the Holy Ghost was present in its greatest fullness before us.

Elder Faber would call on us occasionally and ask us to describe what we were feeling. There were times I couldn't talk or explain my feelings. The spirit was so strong in my heart. There were times I thought, *Is this what it will be like in the presence of my Savior, Jesus Christ?* Indeed, it was a humbling experience and opportunity I would never forget.

The more I learned from this class, the more I tried to implement into my teaching on Sunday. I was delighted on one Sunday when several of the youth commented that I was the best teacher they ever had and loved the way I taught the scriptures and stories. I asked them what made me different from other teachers. They mentioned I used real-life examples and explained the scriptures clearly and made them understandable. I was honored to know they felt that way about me. I knew it was of no effort of my own, but the spirit was teaching the lesson. I was merely an instrument the Lord used to convey His message.

What I came to know in my heart was this group of youth were very talented, special and wanted to learn the gospel and live it. I was so impressed with their testimonies, enthusiasm, and love for the scriptures and their Savior.

I was brokenhearted the day I didn't teach this group any further.

Home Teacher

And visit the house of each member, exhorting them to pray
vocally and in secret and attend to all family duties.

—Doctrine and Covenants 20:51

As a new member of the ward, it seemed as though I was given some
remarkable responsibilities from the onset. I was finding myself
studying more frequently and attending more socials, meetings, and
activities. It was, to be frank, a little overwhelming. When I would
get a little discouraged, there was always someone available to talk to
and discuss my feelings. I became very close to the Elder's Quorum
president and to very good friends from day one.

He invited me to visit with him after church on Sunday. He
told me it would be a brief PPI. I said, "A what?" He said a PPI. I
asked what was that. It sounds scary. He chuckled and told me a PPI
is a personal priesthood interview. I asked him, "How many times do
I have to be interviewed?"

He chuckled again and answered, "The rest of your life."

After church, I met him and we started with a word of prayer,
which he offered. I was relieved, not being comfortable praying in
front of people. He asked me a few questions and then asked if I
would be willing to serve with him in the Elder's Quorum as a home
teacher. Luckily, I knew what a home teaching assignment consisted
of. I told him I would be delighted to serve side by side with him.
Later that evening, he dropped by my house and left me a list of
names with addresses and phone numbers. He told me to ponder

each name and listen for the spirit to give me direction about any of the individuals listed. I said I will do so.

Looking over the list, I did not recognize any of the names. I would not have been able to point them out in church if I had to. Later in the week, I got a phone call from President Packard, and he asked me if I would prepare a ten-minute lesson on the *Ensign* article by the First Presidency. After reading the article, I prepared a lesson for three families we were going to visit. It was at this time the elders came by to say hello and check how I was doing. We talked for a while, and they explained why I was being called on to fulfill so many responsibilities. I walked away with the thought that it is all about my future in the church.

A couple of days later, President Packard picked me up to go home teaching. We had a word of prayer, and off we went. On our way to the first family, he said, "Let me fill you in on these families. All of them are inactive members of the church, they belong to a motorcycle club, have long hair, wear leather jackets, and are very vocal."

I remember wanting to crawl in the trunk of the car and hide the rest of the evening. As the evening came to a rest and we were driving home, President Packard asked me how I felt about the families the Lord has asked us to fellowship and watch over. I told him that now that I have met them and had positive communication, I found myself having a genuine love for them collectively. For nearly a year, we had constant fellowship with these families and some wonderful gospel discussions. Yet again, I was taught the gospel while being "in the service of my fellowman" (Mosiah 2:17).

I recalled the counsel the bishop gave me when I received the priesthood when I read the scripture: "And thus, in their prosperous circumstances, they did not send away any who were naked, or that were hungry, or that were athirst, or that were sick, or that had not been nourished; and they did not set their hearts upon riches; therefore, they were liberal to all, both old and young, both bond and free, both male and female, whether out of the church or in the church, having no respect to persons as to those who stood in need" (Alma 1:30).

It became evident to me both spiritually and temporally that all of God's children are special to Him and I should treat them as Jesus would treat them. My experiences with these three families taught me so much about service to God's children and how precious each one of us are to Him personally.

Personal Priesthood Interview

That as many as shall come before my servants...embracing this calling and commandment, shall be ordained and sent forth to preach the everlasting gospel among the nations.

—Doctrine and Covenants 36:5

Almost a year later after becoming a member of the church, I was home teaching with President Packard, the Elder's Quorum president. On this occasion on the way home, he asked if I had time to come to his home for a personal priesthood interview. I took the invitation as an opportunity to spend more time with such a great mentor, and I was curious what he had up his sleeve for me now.

He invited me into his home office and asked me to be seated. After a moment, we knelt in prayer and he asked for the spirit to be with both of us at this time. Like usual, he asked me a few questions about various topics I was engaged with, such as work, baseball, family, and my calling.

A short time later, he asked me about my personal life and my future and what some of my goals were. He then asked the anxiety-provoking question to me. "Have you ever considered serving a mission?"

My reply was, "Yes. I considered it for about thirty seconds."

He said, "And what did you learn?"

Without hesitation, I quickly said, "It is not for me."

Then he asked me, "Have you prayed about serving a mission?"

And at that moment, my eyes looked down and I began to worry about where this conversation was going.

I replied with a somewhat anxious voice. "No, but I know you want me to." President Packard then counseled with me and gave me some very profound advice and promises to consider. He asked me to go home that night and find a place where I could say my personal prayers out loud but where nobody else could hear me. And he encouraged me "to ask my Heavenly Father whether I should serve a mission for Him at this time in my life." He told me to keep praying and, when I received an answer, to let him know; and whatever came, he would support me fullheartedly.

I returned home and found myself standing inside of the loafing shed where the cows and horses typically spent the night. (Just a side note here, I didn't kneel in prayer for obvious reasons.) I folded my arms, and with all the courage I could muster while feeling some anxiety, I asked my Heavenly Father with sincerity, "Would you support me serving a mission in your vineyard somewhere in the world?" I paused for several moments and waited for further counsel. At that moment, nothing came to my mind. I was drawing a complete blank. So I closed my prayer knowing my answer would eventually come at another time. I was content for the time being.

As I crossed the backyard and began to walk up the back stairs of the deck, I encountered the most tremendous spiritual experience of my life. It was as though a hand was pressing against my chest and I could no longer move forward. I literally felt the physical touch of a hand on my chest but was not able to see anything.

Within seconds of the feeling, I heard a voice speak to me, "If you serve a mission in the Lord's vineyard, your parents will join the church." The experience took less than a minute, but it was so profound and deeply rooted, there was no room for doubt of anxious feelings. It was pure revelation from heaven and as real as the sun shines every day.

The feelings I had were calm, peaceful, and a sense of confidence. All I could do was sit down on the stairs and shed tears of joy. Once again, in just a short time, I had my prayers answered and with such profound direction and guidance. And I knew what I had to do regardless of my personal feelings and thoughts at the time.

Without hesitation, I called President Packard and went and visited him that night. As I revealed to him what I had witnessed, he looked at me and with sincerity said, "I know what you have experienced is true. I feel the spirit testify to me what you have experienced is the truth."

Not long after these amazing miracles unfolded in my life and I knew what God expected of me, I was in the bishop's office having a worthiness interview and preparing to start the process of going on a mission. It was an exciting time in my life, to say the least.

I was so filled with the spirit, I thought my heart was going to burst. The overwhelming feelings were of excitement and then exhaustion over the next several days.

The same night, I received personal revelation. I was in my bedroom and reading before bed. At some point, that same spirit spoke to me again, revealing to me "under no circumstances was I to communicate to my parents what I had experienced with regard to why I was choosing to serve a mission." As quickly as the spirit came, it was gone just as quickly. I knew perfectly well that the Lord had a plan for my parents, but in no manner were they properly prepared at that time.

Over the next several months, I was inspired to share my experiences with a handful of individuals that I trusted and knew would understand the things that had been revealed to me.

President Packard and I drew closer as home teaching companions, as though we were missionary companions. He taught me so much about loving people and seeking opportunities to serve however I could, especially the needy and elderly.

Every day, I thanked my Heavenly Father for the courage and leadership the Elder's Quorum President Ray Packard had to challenge me to ask a simple yet important question of my Heavenly Father. What was more miraculous was the way the answer came and the purpose behind it. I realized my life had made significant changes, and it wasn't over yet.

Stake Conference

And whatsoever city thy servants shall enter, and the people of
that city receive their testimony, let thy peace and thy salvation
be upon that city; that they may gather out of that city the
righteous, that they may come forth to Zion or to her stakes,
the places of thine appointment, with songs of everlasting joy.

—Doctrine and Covenants 109:39

It was just after the first of the year in January of 1982. The phone
rang, and it was the executive secretary of President Frank Wagstaff.
He wanted to know if I could come and meet with the stake president on Sunday morning in his office at the stake center. I mentioned I could do that. For two days, I stewed over what that visit
might consist of and what I was going to be asked to do. My initial
thoughts focused on a calling in the stake and something to do with
the sporting program. I was already involved with playing, coaching,
and officiating in the basketball program.

I arrived early to the stake center on Sunday morning and was
invited to join President Wagstaff in his office. After a short greeting,
he asked that we kneel in prayer and he would offer the prayer. We
took our seats, and he asked a few questions and said he wanted to
ask me a question with regard to the stake conference that was coming in a couple of weeks.

Not knowing where this was headed, he started talking about
how a general authority would be coming to the conference. His
name was Elder Enzio Busche, and he had asked that President

Wagstaff ask a recently new convert in the stake to speak with him for twenty minutes on Sunday morning. I got a lump in my throat, my heart began racing, and my anxiety heightened drastically.

Before I could answer no, President Wagstaff said to me, "Why don't you come sit in this chair?" He laid his hands on my head and pronounced a blessing on me. It was a beautiful blessing, giving me comfort and the intellect to perform my duties and responsibilities when called upon in the church. He blessed me that I would prepare and deliver my comments to those in attendance at stake conference in a manner that would touch hearts, change lives, and strengthen testimonies. I had tears streaming down my face and felt a love from the spirit in a very special way that day. After the blessing, in a loving way, President Wagstaff said, "I assume your answer is yes?" We laughed and hugged each other.

I asked President Wagstaff what the topic was for stake conference, and he asked that I prepare a twenty-minute talk and share my testimony and conversion story. I said it would be an honor to do that. He thanked me, and I went about my day.

Sunday, January 16, 1982, came too fast for me personally. I was excited and nervous about the thought of speaking in a stake conference. After getting to the stake center a half hour early, I joined the Stake Presidency, Elder Busche, and one other speaker. We all knelt in prayer while President Ford offered an inspiring prayer to be with all of us and especially for those who would play a part on the program that morning. We all shook hands and were invited to take our seats on the stand.

I was doing well at first, and the congregation began to get larger in number; and after a few minutes, the chapel, the overflow, and the gym were filled. Brother Fox stood and announced there was overflow seating in the Primary and Relief Society rooms. When I heard that, I began to get nervous and wanted to leave the meeting, knowing Elder Busche could fill my time with no problem.

The opening song was announced along with the opening prayer. The congregation sang, and from my seat, it was beautiful. The opening prayer was edifying, and conference was underway. I was the second speaker on the program followed by a special musical number, followed by a member of the stake presidency. As the first speaker shared their testimony, I quietly asked my Heavenly Father to help me fulfill my responsibility with the task at hand. I had a strong sense of peace, and the spirit was with me.

It was my turn. I gently raised from my seat and moved toward the podium where I felt I had found safety momentarily. I began to open my binder where I had placed my talk and contained the details I wanted to share. Immediately, I felt the Holy Ghost whisper to me to speak from the heart and share my story as it was unfolded to me. I proceeded, and as I did, the words flowed smoothly and I spoke with confidence and with the Spirit. I was greatly humbled, and the message was communicated about how the Lord would have had me deliver. Throughout my talk and on a few occasions, I had to pause to catch my breath because I was so overwhelmed by the spirit that was flowing through me.

After the meeting was over, the Stake Presidency shook my hand and told me I did what they hoped for—a wonderful conversion story with an amazing spirit present. I smiled and said thank you. A moment later, I felt a large hand grip my bicep and pull me in the direction they were standing. It was Elder Enzio Busche! He gave me a big bear hug and said to me, "That was an amazing story and what a miracle you have experienced in your life." He followed up with a promise by saying, "I will see you in the Missionary Training Center (MTC) sometime soon."

It took some time before I was able to get off the stand because people were coming up and saying things like, "Thank you"; "That is an amazing story and experience you have had"; "You brought tears to my eyes." The one that brought tears to my eyes came from a dear friend of mine who said, "Teach me to talk with the spirit and without notes and have the ability to lift and edify hearts, and change people for the good."

It was such a miraculous experience, and I knew again it was nothing I personally did. The Lord used me as an instrument to deliver a story I had had that needed to be communicated to the people of the Spokane East Stake. With faith and a prayer in my heart, I simply opened my mouth, and the Holy Ghost filled it with the words I was to share on that Sabbath Day.

Nine months later, I was in the Missionary Training Center in Provo, Utah. My companion, Elder Hawkins from Colorado, and

I were sharing stories and experiences about life. I shared with him the opportunity I had to speak with Elder Enzio Busche in stake conference and what he promised me about the Missionary Training Center. There was a fireside that evening that all missionaries were to attend. With the missionaries in attendance, we all stood and began to sing "We Thank Thee Oh God for a Prophet." While singing, Elder Busche entered. He would be the speaker that evening. Elder Hawkins turned to me and smiled.

After Elder Busche's comments, he stood on the floor below the podium and shook every missionary's hand. As Elder Hawkins and I approached him, Elder Hawkins told me to remind him of who I was. I grinned. I reached out to shake Elder Busche's hand, and he grabbed me and squeezed my very tightly. He looked at me and said, "Spokane, Washington, stake conference, a new convert."

I was amazed he had remembered, even though he couldn't remember my name. He looked at my name badge and called me Elder Heuett. His love for me and the missionaries radiated in his face, and the aura he had was tremendously overwhelming.

Once again, I had witnessed another miracle in my life, and I had committed myself unto the hands of the Lord. I never forgot why I was serving a mission and the purpose the Lord had for me both personally and in the life of others. I was constantly reminded of my patriarchal blessing: "You shall have the privilege of blessing the lives of many who are inactive and thereby causing that their lives, too, shall be blessed."

And further, "Although no one has mentioned it to you, you know that you have been selected to be a representative in your family both to those who have died and thus not received the blessings of the gospel, and equally as important, to those who are yet living and who will yet live, because you are the key to their eternal salvation."

Through these amazing experiences and blessings, I had been privy to growing quickly in the gospel, doing the Lord's work in His vineyard, and fulfilling my responsibilities. How grateful I was for President Frank Wagstaff to give me the opportunity to speak in the stake conference that extended beyond the podium that day.

Melchizedek Priesthood

And this greater priesthood administereth the gospel
and holdeth the key of the mysteries of the kingdom,
even the key of the knowledge of God.

—Doctrine and Covenants 84:19

Another milestone in my life came on June 9, 1982, when Brother George Gary Bishop laid his hands on my head and ordained me to the office of an elder in the Melchizedek Priesthood. The ordination took place in the home of the Bishop family. Along with Brother Bishop, standing in the circle were Bishop Scott; Brother Davenport of the bishopric; President Wagstaff of the stake presidency; his two counselors, Brother Foxx and Ford; and the Bishop family. They were all in attendance.

I remember well the spirit that was present during the ordination and being filled with love from those who participated in the ordination. President Wagstaff took a few minutes and taught the importance of being ordained an elder in the Melchizedek Priesthood. It was an honor to be ordained an elder in the church knowing that my priesthood responsibilities would be magnified. The overwhelming feeling of the spirit lingered with me most of the day and into the evening whenever I thought of the event that happened to me that day.

The next several days were somewhat unusual to me, mostly in Spirit, and the changes I was experiencing in my internal feelings. I became more conscientious of my surroundings, how I approached my prayers, the way I studied the scriptures—things seemed to have a purpose with deeper meaning and understanding. It was a feeling of great power and strength and a feeling that was difficult to explain. But it was there and noticeable.

The Temple

Wherefore, stand ye in holy places, and be not
moved, until the day of the Lord come; for behold
it cometh quickly, saith the Lord, Amen.

—Doctrine and Covenants 87:8

I was interviewed by Bishop Scott on September 7, 1982, for my temple recommend and worthiness. On September 21, 1982, President Wagstaff interviewed me and found me worthy to receive my recommend and participate in the temple ordinances.

When it was time for me to go to the temple and participate in the temple ordinances, it was the most exciting time of my life. The closest temple to Spokane Valley where I lived was the Seattle, Washington, temple roughly six hours away. It was an honor to be traveling with several members of the ward, including the Bishop Scott, his wife, Sister Bishop, Brother Gary Scott, who was attending the temple for the first time.

One of the highlights of the day came about two hours out of Spokane when Brother Scott, the bishop's son, was pulled over for speeding. It became a humorous moment after the officer was gone and we headed down the highway.

After a good night's sleep, we entered the temple gate and onto the temple grounds. It was serene, sporting some of the most beautiful flowers, shrubs, and trees found anywhere on earth. I remember standing next to Sister Bishop and telling her how magnificent the temple looked. I succumbed to the presence of the spirit instantly and was overwhelmed with the power of the Holy Ghost. The temple itself was magnificent in size and beauty. I could feel the spirit very strongly and just wanted to take the moment and ponder the eternal perspective of what was going to happen on this day.

On October 9, 1982, I entered the Seattle temple where things were moving rapidly and was intimidating. But I had an escort that was right by my side the whole time. There were several steps I had to be part of that I am not able to share or discuss here in this book. What I can tell you is there is no other place on earth where a person can feel closer to God and Jesus Christ than in the temple. The experience was remarkable. It humbled me, and I knew there would never be a greater work that I was part of than the day I became an endowed member of the Church of Jesus Christ of Latter-day Saints.

I knew the covenants and promises I made in the temple that day were real, eternal, and provided a perspective of what God's true teachings involved here on earth and throughout the eternities.

I continue to be amazed with how much God truly loves us and what He gives us daily to enjoy life and prepare to return and live with Him. It is my prayer that I live worthy of His blessings and teachings to encounter Him in His kingdom and have what he has prepared for me.

All the spiritual experiences that I had had to that moment— none were more spiritual in power, strength, inspiration, and God's eternal glory than what I felt internally and externally at the temple that day.

Mission Call

Lift up your heart and rejoice, for the hour of your mission is come.

—Doctrine and Covenants 31:3

On September 2, 1982, I received my mission call to serve in the Des Moines, Iowa, mission. I was to report on October 28, 1982, to the Missionary Training Center in Provo, Utah.

Those that were there when I opened the envelope were my parents, members of the Bishop family, and my siblings. It was a time of great excitement for me personally. I was not overly excited to be leaving home, but I knew what blessings were going to be in store for me and eventually my family.

It was truly a feeling of sacrifice for me personally. Currently, my parents, mostly my dad, was not very supportive of my decision to leave home. They didn't really understand why I was going on a mission. I had received instructions through the spirit not to divulge any information to my parents about the revelations I had been privy to because of their lack of understanding.

Before opening the envelope, I was nervous, wondering where the Lord was sending me to serve in His vineyard. The spirit that came over me as I read the following: "You are hereby called to serve as a missionary of The Church of Jesus Christ of Latter-day Saints to labor in the Iowa Des Moines Mission." It was a tremendous feeling of gratification and willingness.

Once the mission location was revealed to me, I was calm, and I knew this would be a great opportunity for me. I also knew my parents would be comforted knowing I was not going to some foreign country far away.

We pulled out the road atlas, looked up the state of Iowa, and started locating where Des Moines was in the state. Over the next couple of days, I did research to learn about the state of Iowa historically, the culture of the Midwest, and of course what sports teams they had both at the collegiate level and pro level if there were any at the time.

The day after my call came in the mail, I signed the acceptance letter, filled out some forms, and sent it back to the Missionary Department in Salt Lake City, Utah. It was then I really realized the commitment I had made to myself, my family, and the Lord. The prayer I offered months earlier, personal revelation, and all that I had experienced had led up to this one great event the Lord had in store for me the whole time.

It was really happening, and my emotions were like a roller-coaster ride each day for the next month. But I had committed into the Lord's hands, and I never forgot what I needed to do. Once the communication was out to the ward members, the bishop, the stake president, and other people were excited for me. I received phone calls, visits by individuals, and felt like a celebrity at church, which I was nowhere close to being. But I must admit I did enjoy the excitement others had for me, much more than the attention I received.

The next several weeks were extremely busy, trying to get ready to leave home. I had my wisdom teeth pulled, went to the doctor for a few shots that were required, finished up working at my job, and spent time with family and friends. Buying clothes and books that were recommended and planning meetings that had to take place with church leaders, it was an exciting but hectic time all in just a short period.

Mission Departure

And faith, hope, charity and love, with an eye single
to the glory of God, qualify him for the work.

—Doctrine and Covenants 4:5

Time was going quickly, and I found myself preparing to leave home
and put what I knew as my life behind me and serve the Lord in His
vineyard. Sunday morning arrived, and it would be the last sacrament meeting I would attend in the Eight ward for some time.

While sitting on the stand and watching the good saints file
into the chapel and find their seats, memories flooded my mind that
I had experienced with almost every one of them in some capacity.
They were my dearest friends who spent countless hours fellowshipping me, teaching me, training me for the very moment that had
arrived, and simply loving me in a Christlike manner.

I would be forever grateful for the good people they are and
prayed the Lord would bless them in abundance. I was doing well
until Brother Perks came to the front of the chapel, leaned over the
short wall where I was sitting, and asked, "How are you doing?" I
choked up and couldn't talk. He understood and returned to his seat.

After the blessing and passing of the sacrament, a member of
the bishopric stood and announced the services for the meeting.
When it was my turn to speak, I arose from my seat and walked to
the podium. I had a heavy heart knowing it was the last time I would
see some of these good people. Some would move away, some would
pass through life, and others would most likely be in another ward

when I return home. I truly felt a Christlike love for these people whom I considered my friends.

I shared a few comments with the congregation about changes that I had experienced over the last year since becoming a member of the Church of Jesus Christ of Latter-day Saints. My comments were focused on experiences playing church sports but more in the spiritual realm of things, such as home teaching, teaching the gospel, learning principles of the gospel, and the fellowshipping I had received from the entire ward.

Toward the end of my comments, I reminded the congregation why I was going on a mission. That if I did, my parents would join the church. I never received how they would join, when they would convert, who would be pivotal in their life at the time; I just trusted and knew the Lord would bring it to pass.

I asked the entire ward not to reveal to my parents why I was going to serve the Lord. I communicated to the members my parents were not very happy with my decision and did not understand, but the day would come when it would be revealed to them.

With tears in my eyes, I closed my comments with my testimony and thanked them all for all their support and wonderful examples to me.

Missionary Setting Apart

We believe that a man must be called of God, by prophecy,
and by the laying on of hands by those who are in authority, to
preach the Gospel and administer in the ordinances thereof.

—Articles of Faith 5

On October 23, 1982, I was set apart by President Frank Wagstaff
at the stake center. At that moment forth, I carried the missionary
mantle and was to keep all mission rules. I don't recollect all that was
mentioned in the blessing, but I know it was powerful and it came
from my Heavenly Father. It was direct in what I should do and what
was expected of me.

I do remember that I would be blessed by teaching the gospel to
many and witnessing them entering the waters of baptism and that
I would have the opportunity of bringing many who were inactive
back to the church that they might have blessings that their Heavenly
Father had in store for them. I would have several missionary companions and love them and be an example in the work I was called to
do. And lastly, that through my service, my family would be greatly
blessed.

In attendance were my parents, my brother Steve, and members
of the Bishop family.

Trip to Provo, Utah

We have traveled from house to house, relying upon
the mercies of the world—not upon the mercies of
the world alone but upon the mercies of God.

—Alma 26:28

I woke up early on the morning of October 26, 1982. I went upstairs
to say goodbye to my dad who was leaving for work. I walked into
the kitchen, and he was leaning on my mom and crying on her
shoulder. That was the first time I ever witnessed my dad crying in
that capacity. My stomach knotted up as I turned to walk into the
bathroom. I closed the bathroom door and broke into tears myself.
I asked myself, *What am I doing?* For a split second, I had a second
thought but quickly recaptured the commitment I had made to the
Lord. I uttered a prayer and prepared for the rest of the day.

I left home with my mom and Sister Jan Bishop and headed for
Provo, Utah. We arrived in the late afternoon, and I met with Art
Hansen who was attending BYU and stayed at his apartment.

The next day, I went to class with my mom, Jan Bishop, and
Janet Bishop. It was an interesting class and packed full of students.
Afterward, we all went to lunch and toured the BYU campus. We
drove up to Provo temple grounds and enjoyed the beauty there of the
Lord's House. Later in the evening, we went to dinner at Magleby's
restaurant and had a great dinner and visit. Most of the discussion
was focused on my feelings of leaving for my mission. I found myself
getting nervous of the impact it would have on me, my family, and

friends. I was able to capture my composure by saying a quiet prayer and enjoying the time with those who were with me.

I was very tired at the end of the day and actually slept quite well.

The Missionary Training Center

Behold, I sent you out to testify and warn the people, and it becometh every man who hath been warned to warn his neighbor.

—Doctrine and Covenants 88:81

The morning of October 28, 1982, at nine, I entered the Missionary Training Center (MTC) in Provo, Utah. My mom, Sister Jan Bishop, and Art Hansen were all there by my side. After brief instruction from the Missionary Training Center president, the missionaries were to say their goodbyes to family and friends and exit the room out behind a designated wall where they would receive further instruction. Everyone was in tears, but I was able to stay composed. I knew what I was doing, and it was for a marvelous work to come forth at some point.

I hugged each one of them and told them I loved them. My mom took advantage to give me some motherly advice before I was not in her presence for a while. She told me I better keep my white shirts cleaned and pressed and never send home a picture wearing a wrinkled shirt. I promised her to keep myself groomed and well-dressed.

When Elder Art Hansen hugged me, I got a little emotional. We had become such good friends, and he played such a significant role in my life during his time as a missionary. I told him I would try to do everything possible to be a missionary like he was. He answered back and told me I would be a much better missionary than he was.

I thanked him for all he had done for me, and I would forever be grateful for him.

I approached the wall I was to walk around into a hallway and wanted to turn and look back one more time. But the spirit directed my thoughts and actions to move forward and not look back. I went around the corner into a large hallway where I was directed to move to the tables ahead. Once there, I received instructions with regard to mealtimes, a room key, the name of the building I would be living in the next few weeks for training, and the name of my companion, along with a binder of more instructions.

I found my room, unlocked the door, opened it up, and found a missionary in the room. Elder McKim from California was waiting for his companion to show up. I picked out my bed, unpacked my belongings, organized my desk, and waited patiently for my companion to show up. Elder McKim's companion, Elder Pratt, from Utah made his way to the room; and shortly thereafter, Elder Hawkins from Colorado, my companion, made his appearance. Within minutes, we were all friends and excited to be serving our mission. By bedtime, we all had shared with one another why we decided to go on a mission. It was interesting and unique to hear the different testimonies of why each of us decided to leave our families and come serve the Lord.

The first night in the Missionary Training Center, we got the eight missionaries assigned to our district and went to the cafeteria for dinner. It was almost like we had all been friends for life, yet we all had a different background.

Toward bedtime, I looked out the window of my dorm room and saw the lights shining on the BYU football field. When I saw the lights, I began to reflect on my mom and Sister Bishop who had been traveling home during the day. I said a quiet prayer for their safe return home.

At bedtime, I was exhausted from the emotions that had raced through me over the last several hours. I knelt in prayer at ten in the evening and crawled into my bed and fell asleep.

My third day in the Missionary Training Center, I received my first letter. It was from Sister Bishop, and I was so excited to hear from someone on the outside walls of the Missionary Training Center. Her letter surprised me greatly and brought a couple of tears to my eyes as I read it. She mentioned in her letter when my mom and her started the journey home from Provo, Utah, to Spokane, Washington, another miracle was unfolding. I was busy becoming acquainted with the Missionary Training Center, attending classes, and spending hours studying scriptures and missionary discussions we would use in the mission field.

As they approached Salt Lake City, Sister Jan Bishop asked my mom if she would like to see temple square and take a short tour. My mom was delighted in the offer, and the two of them enjoyed the spirit of temple square. Sister Bishop later wrote me expressing that my mom said, "Who knows before Brian gets home, we may all be members." Sister Bishop wrote in her letter how excited my mom's comment made her. I could only smile and give thanks to my Heavenly Father and my Savior Jesus Christ.

On the second week of the MTC, I was invited to meet with the MTC president. We had a short visit, and he extended an opportunity to me to serve as the district leader of the group of missionaries I was serving with at the time. I accepted, and he and a counselor set me apart for the calling. I was honored for this chance simply because as a recent convert to the church, I felt so inadequate to the other missionaries who seemed more qualified. But it was a blessing in my life at that time because I was able to help some of the elders who were struggling with homesickness, testimonies, and other items like, you know, girlfriends.

I came to love each of those elders and sisters in our district. They were hardworking, faithful, and had strong testimonies to share with people. We exceled in our learning and advanced as young missionaries quickly in our preparation to enter the field of work in the Des Moines, Iowa, mission. I witnessed miracles from giving priesthood blessings, fasting and praying, and sharing my testimony with others during this time.

I remember going to bed some nights with tears in my eyes from knowing of the pain, uncertainties, and feelings some of the other missionaries shared with me. I knew of their fears and struggles but was in no way going to let them quit. When it was time to fly to Des Moines, Iowa, we were all there prepared and ready to go to work in the Lord's vineyard.

The morning I was packing and preparing to get on the bus to go to the airport, I was reminded of the wonderful experience the MTC brought to me. I had made new friends, gained leadership experience, prepared myself efficiently, and had many spiritual experiences that would have a lasting impact on me for a lifetime.

Again, I was moving onto bigger and more important things as a missionary. It was time to put what I had learned to work and show the Lord "I had committed myself into His Hands."

Sacrifices

Thou shalt offer a sacrifice unto the Lord thy God in righteousness, even that of a broken heart and a contrite spirit.

—Doctrine and Covenants 59:8

When I left home, I had enough money to pay for the Missionary Training Center and three months in the mission field. I bought my mission clothes at a secondhand store, except one tie that Elder Hansen gave to me (which I still have to this day). I survived on a meager income as missionaries do.

During the second month of my mission, my bishop called me and asked how I was paying for my mission. I told him that I had enough for one more month of provisions and that I would have no more money. He began to cry over the phone and asked me how I was going to survive after that financially. I told him that I figured the Lord would take care of it. I was reminded of a scripture at the time: "And thou shalt take no purse nor script, neither staves, neither two coats, for the church shall give unto thee in the very hour what thou needest for food and for raiment, and for shoes and for money, and for script" (Doctrine and Covenants 24:18).

My bishop told me he would get back in touch with me. A few weeks later, I received a letter from the mission president that my missionary funds were being taken care of and that I would be able to continue my service. I later found out that the high priest of my home ward provided the monthly funds for my mission. I was so grateful and blessed for my decisions.

I made the decision to put myself "in His hands" and go forward with faith and nothing wavering, and the Lord would take care of me.

I had turned away from the things I loved most at the time: my friends, family, playing baseball, leaving all that I knew behind to serve the Lord, a much greater sacrifice with greater blessings in store.

Personally, the greatest sacrifice I knew that had been made was not by me at all. I was reaping the opportunities and blessings of a sacrifice far greater than I could give. I was making choices to serve the Lord because of the sacrifices He made in my behalf. Every day, I tried hard to remember the Savior in the Garden of Gethsemane while He took upon Himself the sins of every man, woman, and child who would live on this earth. And while He suffered on the cross and gave His life for us all, He became Jesus the Christ.

I realized the sacrifices I was making were significant, but I wasn't sure of the entire purpose of my sacrifices. At times, I felt sad because I knew I was being selfish rather than focusing on what was important with the errand I was asked to perform—serve for the Lord. And in doing so, He would take care of His children that I crossed paths with, including my parents and family.

Humbling myself and through sincere prayer, I forgot myself and went to work. The blessings that came were remarkable and not without knowing they were from the Lord. I had come to know what it meant to be a true disciple and missionary of Jesus Christ.

It was an experience I will remember as long as I live.

Parents' Conversion

O all ye that are spared because ye were more righteous
than they, will ye not now return unto me, and repent
of your sins, and be converted, that I may heal you.

—3 Nephi 9:13

On February 27, 1983, at one in the morning, the phone rang. Elder
King, my companion, answered; and I heard him say, "Just a minute
please. Elder Heuett, it is for you."

When I answered, I heard my mom say, "I have tried calling all
day. Where have you been?" After explaining to her what I had been
doing, she replied with, "I called to tell you I was baptized today." My
heart swelled with joy, my eyes filled with tears, and I knew that God
had fulfilled part of His promise.

My mom and I visited for a few minutes and asked her why she
had not mentioned to me she was investigating the church. I asked
her what brought this occasion to the forefront of her life? She said
after she got home from taking me to the Missionary Training Center
in Provo, Utah, and touring Temple Square in Salt Lake City, Utah,
she told my dad that if something like a mission and leaving home
was so important to me, maybe they need to check into it.

She told me that she and my dad met with the full-time missionaries and, at one point, with Bishop Scott. During these visits, my dad
told them he did not want anything communicated to me that they were
going to investigate the teachings of the Church of Jesus Christ of Latter-
day Saints. And if anyone leaked it to me, all meetings would cease.

I told her that her heart was touched by the spirit in the Missionary Training Center and by being on temple square. She expressed some emotions, and I communicated to her my love for her and the choice she made to become a member of the only true church on earth. She thanked me and told me to get back to bed. I laughed, and we hung up the phone.

Elder King and I went to the twenty-four-hour convenient store and bought root beer, ice cream, and plastic cups and came home and celebrated the occasion with root beer floats and eggs and bacon.

On March 3, 1983, the phone rang, and I answered to my dad's voice letting me know he entered the waters of baptism that morning. Heavenly Father had kept his promise, and I felt the blessings of the gospel spreading among my own family members. I was so overcome with joy, I could hardly contain myself.

I asked my dad why he didn't get baptized with mom. He said he was a little more stubborn and was not done running the missionaries through the ringer. That was so much my dad, having things done his way, on his time, and making sure every facet of investigation was taught and he understood it. I learned through letters later that he gave the elders a real run for their money during the discussions and seeking answers to the scriptures and gospel topics. For some reason, I was not surprised and felt honored I was not there. It became clear why the Lord placed me in the cornfields of Iowa so I would not interfere with His work on the home front.

After hanging up the phone, I called my mission president and told him of the excitement that had been communicated to me. I told him my mission was fulfilled and I could go home. He said to me, "Elder Heuett, there are others who are prepared for you to teach and bring the blessings of the gospel to them. Now go find them. Have a nice day too!"

I was reminded of the scripture: "Go ye therefore, and teach all nations, baptizing them in the name of the Father, and of the Son, and of the Holy Ghost: Teaching them to observe all things whatsoever I have commanded you: and, lo, I am with you always, even unto the end of the world. Amen" (Matthew 28: 19–20).

Return with Honor and Glory

For therein are the keys of the holy priesthood
ordained, that you may receive honor and glory.

—Doctrine and Covenants 124:34

On May 12, 1984, I left the mission home with President and Sister
Van Tassell and the other missionaries that I served with in the
Missionary Training Center. The missionaries were all on the same
flight from Des Moines, Iowa, to Denver, Colorado. Ironically, it came
to an end, so to speak, like it started. When we left the Missionary
Training Center, I loaded the van for the airport last to make sure the
other missionaries were all accounted for. In Denver, I was the last
to board my connecting flight onto Spokane, Washington. All the
missionaries had made their connecting flights and headed home to
their families waiting excitedly.

On my flight from Denver to Spokane, I had some time to
reflect on my mission, my companions, people I had taught the gospel to and witnessed their conversion to baptism. I thought of Sister
Larkin who was baptized and later served her own mission. After
about an hour, a young lady sitting next to me noticed my name
badge and asked me if I was an LDS missionary. I confirmed with
her, which led to an hour-long discussion of the gospel. She was
attending college in Helena, Montana, at the time and had three
LDS roommates. I left her with a copy of the Book of Mormon,
some pamphlets, my missionary card, and told her when she gets

back to Helena, to let her roommates know she wants to investigate the church. She promised me she would do so.

For some reason, when the pilot came on the speaker and asked the stewardess to prepare for landing into the Spokane airport, I got nervous, more nervous than when I left for my mission. I started to evaluate why I felt the emotions I was feeling.

I left with parents wanting nothing to do with my mission and not understanding the what, why, and when of serving a mission. I couldn't communicate the details of why I was serving; I was forbidden at the time. But it became clear to them four months after I left home.

Now, I was about twenty minutes from landing in my home city where I was born and raised to return into the arms of family and friends. One of the airline stewardesses asked me if I was going to wait and exit the plane last. I mentioned to her that is my full purpose. She laughed saying, "All you missionaries are just alike." I laughed!

It took about fifteen minutes to unload the passengers from the plane, and it was my turn to walk the aisle of the plane and down the ramp to the foyer of the airport. When I came into sight of those waiting, it was such an exciting feeling. There was a sign being held that said, "Welcome home Elder Heuett." Things felt different. I felt different from when I left home. My parents were smiling, and my mom was weeping in my arms while telling me she was so glad I was home. There were several individuals there who had played a significant role in my conversion and in the conversion of my parents.

The rest of the day, I felt lost and lonely, somewhat down and without energy. I read the scriptures and visited with my mom. My dad was working. My siblings were all on their own by now and working or going to school. In the early evening, President Frank Wagstaff stopped by the house, and he and I visited in the family room. He asked about my mission and then released me as a full-time missionary. I have to say, it was the worst moment I ever had since joining the church. I felt like someone put their hand down my throat and ripped my heart out. The missionary mantle was gone in just seconds. It left me weak physically and spiritually drained. I knew that the missionary protection and inspiration had departed from me.

That night, when I went to my bedroom and prepared to retire for the night, I found myself alone on my knees preparing for prayer. Only this time, there was no companion, just me. My emotions took over for a few minutes, and the thought came to me that I was not alone. From the invitation to hear the gospel to the present moment, God and Jesus Christ had always been with me. Why not now? I realized that I had spent time teaching about a man, Jesus Christ, who had experienced loneliness in the most difficult times. He understood me and my current situation; and the strength gained from this thought provided the energy to pray more intently, with more desire, and with more love for my Savior.

Later in the evening, my mom came to check on me. That moment, I broke down emotionally and told her I was having a difficult time coming home. I loved my mission so much and didn't want to leave. Somehow in a mother's way, she understood and had the words I needed to hear for comfort and adjustment. The next couple of days, I spent staying busy around the house. I tilled the garden for my dad until the engine seized because there was no oil in the tiller. I was not used to eating and not preparing my own meals. But my mom's cooking was divine. I read my scriptures and wrote in my missionary journal about the last few days in the mission field prior to coming home.

On Sunday, I stood on the same podium I spoke from when I left. This time, there was no heavy heart or sadness. It was with honor, joy, love, and excitement for all the change that had taken place while I was gone serving the Lord. This time when I looked over the congregation, I witnessed two people whom I loved so much, my parents, sitting in the pews; and I knew they were there because the Lord promised they would be.

The bishop asked me to take about twenty minutes and report on my mission and some of the experiences I had while serving the Lord. After introducing myself to the new members of the ward whom I did not know prior to leaving, I gave a report of some of my experiences that meant the most to me. I talked about some of the converts that I taught the gospel to and some of my companions. Then, I turned my focus to my parents and revealed to them and the ward why I chose to serve a mission and had to keep it confidential, really between the Lord and I and a few others that were close to me.

It was with honor and glory that I stood and concluded the story I had started with so many months prior. It was not sacrifice as much as it was honor and glory that the Lord led me by the hand and taught me what was important for myself while He prepared what was important for my parents and, later, other members of my family.

At the podium that day, my testimony was sealed when the spirit conveyed to me that "into His hands I commit" was always my goal and what mattered most in my life.

To this day, I would do it all again if the chance ever presented itself. I learned during this time in my life that the Lord works in mysterious ways; and He counsels us, "My thoughts are not your thoughts, neither are your ways my ways, saith the Lord. For as the heavens are higher than your ways, and my thoughts than your thoughts" (Isaiah 55: 8–9).

It was with honor and glory that I was invited by a righteous priesthood holder, President Packard, to pray and ask a simple question of my Heavenly Father; and with a perfect plan in place, God answered what I must do. It was with that same honor and glory I fulfilled what was expected of me and, in and of itself, brought honor and glory.

Into His Hands I Commit

Commit thy works unto the Lord, and thy
thoughts shall be established.

—Proverbs 16:3

Throughout scripture, we are taught that all things are in the hand of God. He has in His hand the "heavens and earth" (Doctrine and Covenants 67:16). We learn that "all flesh is in the Lord's hand" (Doctrine and Covenants 101:16). I learned by committing to the gospel of Jesus Christ that God truly controls all things by His hand. And if we are "humble, the Lord shall lead thee by thy hand" (Doctrine and Covenants 112:10).

Learning this eternal principle through reading the scriptures, attending church on Sunday, going to Sunday school and priesthood classes, having discussions with those who understood the scriptures enlightened my mind of this mortal experience and the immortal experience that would eventually come for all of us. Through humble, sincere prayer, I learned that God really does have control and blesses us individually when we keep His commandments and live righteously.

While growing up, I attended several different religious denominations from time to time with my family. I found myself attending the St. Lutheran church with my siblings and cousins frequently. We were all baptized on a Sunday by sprinkling of water on the head. All of us received a new Bible and were more excited about that than being baptized. In part, the table was set for what was to come years later in my religious life.

After the invitation to learn of the LDS church and reading the scriptures, I realized in a short time that what I was being taught was different from anything else I ever heard or read. Having the Book of Mormon as a second witness of Jesus Christ and knowing through prayer it was true and the words of God and His son Jesus Christ, I committed fullheartedly, nothing wavering, with no second thoughts of which religion I wanted to be a part of.

When I committed my life "into His hands," it became apparent to me that all Christian sects were good and taught some truths of God's plan but not in a complete fullness of what the Church of Jesus Christ of Latter-day Saints taught. It was embedded into my soul and became part of who I was. My commitment into the Lord's hand brought a deeper understanding of the scriptures, the characteristics of Jesus Christ, and some of the mysteries of the kingdom of God began to unfold to me even at an early stage of my commitment and conversion. The Holy Ghost revealed to me earthly and heavenly truths in a very clear and precise manner. I knew my heart had experienced a mighty change and it would be with me through my life and throughout the eternities.

The next year as a convert to the Church I experienced some of the best times of my life at that time. I developed magnificent friendships in the Church through sports, Ward and Stake activities, attending Church meetings, home teaching, but none were more important than the time I spent by myself reading the scriptures, and other good books, and kneeling in prayer.

It was during this time that I developed a love for the prophet Joseph Smith Jr. and the experiences he had restoring the gospel back to the earth. In many ways, I felt a deep and genuine connection to him. He too, as I did, investigated many religious sects, read the Bible, prayed when he had questions about religion, and consulted with his parents. And of course, he played sporting games with all the kids that lived nearby.

All these things were significant parts of my willingness to "commit myself into His Hands." There never was a time in my life

I was happier and felt so inspired as I did at this time. What I didn't realize was where all this was leading me.

At the same time, I was being tested greatly by some of the most important issues in my life. I had to make decisions that were tough for me to make. I knew I was being tested and the Lord wanted to see how "committed to Him" I would be.

The first difficult decision confronting me was the comments and harassment I was getting from some of my closest friends. I grew up with these individuals and we were very close friends, but they began to call me a "religious man," accusing me of belonging and worshipping a "cult," calling me a "Bible basher," and telling me I had become a religious freak. I was deeply wounded, offended, and scared from these kinds of harsh words and behaviors. They certainly made me feel as though I had forsaken them and we could no longer be friends.

The second difficult decision I had to make focused on what I enjoyed doing the most in my life, playing baseball. I was playing for a semipro team where I was in the pitching rotation, trying to break into baseball as a career. The difficulty with this was we played doubleheaders on Saturday and Sunday each weekend. The team expected me to be there, and unfortunately, I could not make that commitment. With a heavy heart and deep sadness, I shared with one of my best friends and player/coach I would not be attending Sunday games. It caused some hard feelings, and I decided to take a break away from the game I enjoyed so much.

During this time, I turned toward two of my dearest acquaintances in the church; the first was Brother Perks. Without going into much detail, I mentioned to him how some of my friends were treating me. He sat down with me, encouraged me, and shared with me that as I would change, my friends would change too. He told me not to be afraid of the pathway I had chosen to follow and live and that it would bring me more happiness than anything else I committed to. He helped me understand what was important, and he and I developed a lifelong friendship.

The second individual was Sister Jan Bishop. She and her family played such a significant role in fellowshipping me in the gospel from the very beginning. I enjoyed being with the Bishop family and spending time with them. There was a tremendous love between the family members, a love of the gospel, and they lived a life I wanted to emulate for myself. I was visiting with Sister Bishop on a Sunday and mentioned to her I was going through some difficult times. She immediately found her scriptures and turned to a verse in the Doctrine and Covenants and had me read it. The verse is as follows: "For after much tribulation come the blessings. Wherefor the day cometh that ye shall be crowned with much glory; and the hour is not yet, but, is nigh at hand" (Doctrine and Covenants 58:4).

After reading the verse of scripture, I realized what I must do with regard to my friendships and decisions with playing baseball. My heart was in both places, but as the scriptures teach us, "No man can serve two masters; either he will hate the one, and, love the other; or else he will hold to the one, and despise the other. Ye cannot serve God and mammon" (Matthew 6: 24). I realized that my testimony was embedded deep into my heart and that God the Father and Jesus Christ loved me and had a special role for me to play in the coming months. I knew I had "committed into His Hands."

The first year and few months as a convert of the Church of Jesus Christ of Latter-day Saints was a tremendous experience. I experienced divine revelation on several occasions, solidified my testimony of the gospel in every facet, developed friendships that would last through the eternities, and learned to speak with the spirit to lift others' souls.

Personally, I made the choice to come "into His Hands" through gaining a testimony of the greatest message of our time that Joseph Smith Jr. is a living prophet and he did see God the Father and Jesus Christ. He restored the priesthood and ordinances in the last days so the church could grow and flourish throughout the world. He translated the most correct book on earth, the Book of Mormon, another testament of Jesus Christ.

Through prayer and scriptures, I developed a personal knowledge of who Christ is and established a personal relationship with Him. Through prayer and scripture reading, I learned to recognize the Holy Ghost and how it speaks and communicates to me. The importance of serving others and being served is part of the gospel plan, and that includes home teaching and ministering.

Lastly, my most cherished moment came one Saturday when I was at home in my own house, sitting in a chair and pondering things in life and analyzing my goals and aspirations. I had been out of high school a little over a year. I had given up a full-ride baseball scholarship, working in a dead-end job, and not really having any direction at that time. When I was about to sink into despair, the spirit came over me and testified that God loved me, I was one of His spirit sons, and He had a plan for me. I became very emotional; it was as though He was right there in the room with me. I suddenly felt strengthened and edified in the spirit and knew something was coming.

The experiences contained in this book played a very real and significant part of my ability to come "into His Hands I commit."

Personal Testimony

For the testimony of Jesus is the spirit of prophecy.

—Revelation 19:10

Since the day I was invited to investigate the Church of Jesus Christ of Latter-day Saints, I have been developing my personal testimony of the gospel. The reader must understand that a testimony comes from having experiences and learning principles of the gospel. For example, paying tithing, keeping the Word of Wisdom, knowing Joseph Smith Jr. is a prophet of God, the Book of Mormon is true, and so on.

There must be a level of faith acquired by the person wanting to know what is true or not. Humble, sincere prayer must be an inspirational part of developing a personal testimony. Lastly, a person needs to live and keep the commandments of God by acting on what they know to be the truth. I came to know the power of tithing and the blessings that come from paying tithing, especially the spiritual blessings by paying a faithful tithe and fast offerings. The same goes for any commandment; you want to know for a surety of the truthfulness of a commandment then live it daily.

A testimony of the gospel is the "sure knowledge, received by revelation from the Holy Ghost, of the divinity of the work in the latter-days. A testimony consists of knowledge that comes by revelation, such as knowing Jesus is the Christ. A testimony is developed when the Holy Ghost speaks to the spirit within men; it comes when the whisperings of the still small voice are heard by the inner man" (Mormon Doctrine, 785).

I have been privileged during my conversion years to the Church of Jesus Christ of Latter-day Saints, including my mission period, to come to a completeness of my testimony. I have witnessed, been a part of, and been on the receiving end of what it means to have a testimony of the gospel. For me, it happened when I came to understand the gospel is about a few fundamental principles that Christ expects of me.

One, that I personally know that Jesus Christ is the Son of God and the Savior of the world (Doctrine and Covenants 46:13); two, Joseph Smith Jr. is a prophet of God, who restored the gospel in the last dispensation; and three, the Church of Jesus Christ of Latter-day Saints is "the only true and living church on the face of the whole earth" (Doctrine and Covenants 1:30).

There are other obligations that I have come to have a personal testimony of as a convert to the church. Having a testimony of the gospel is knowing through the spirit that it is my obligation to share and bear witness of the sacredness of the Lord's work here on earth. Part of our baptism covenant is always to stand as a witness of God in all places, at all times, and in all things. For me, I have tried to testify when appropriate and the time is right to others of the witness I have of the gospel. Perform missionary work to those seeking the Lord in their life. Minister to the needy, those who seek repentance, and especially the elderly when possible. And certainly, be prepared to perform priesthood responsibilities to those who stand in need of righteous help in any capacity.

It has been with great excitement, hard work, personal patience, and encouragement from others that this book has come to fruition. My testimony has been strengthened while writing and sharing my personal experiences of my conversion and learning the phrase of "into His hands I commit." Since my early years as a member of the Lord's church, I have been honored to be blessed with pure knowledge of what was once my testimony of the gospel. It has been through the revelation of the Holy Ghost that has communicated to my heart what the eternal truths of the gospel are. I know without any doubt, nothing wavering in my own heart and knowledge that all things pertaining to the gospel in this simple book are true and a part of my personal life.

At this time, I want to share what I have come to learn and understand as pure knowledge and testimony of the gospel. In my life, I have come to know when I seek forgiveness of my misgivings, repent properly of my weaknesses, and live my life as a true disciple of Jesus Christ, my testimony increases twofold; and my knowledge, which consist of the mysteries of the kingdom of God, begin to unfold to me spiritually.

There is no greater feeling in life than to go throughout a day with confidence and happiness in all I do, seeking the opportunity to share the gospel or serve someone less fortunate, teaching a Sunday school lesson, having sincere prayer, seeking understanding of the scriptures and having them open up to me, and at the end of the day, knowing for a surety that the Holy Ghost was with you all day and that the angels in heaven were watching over me.

I testify that the Church of Jesus Christ of Latter-day Saints is the only true church on the earth, Jesus is the Christ and Savior of the world, God holds us in His hands, the Holy Ghost bears truth of all things, Joseph Smith Jr. is God's prophet who restored the gospel and its ordinances to the earth in these the latter days, and the Book of Mormon is another testament of Jesus Christ and the most correct of any book on earth.

It is my sincere desire and prayer that those who are searching for the true religion on the earth and desiring to have a personal relationship with Christ will turn their hearts to the Church of Jesus Christ of Latter-day Saints. Those who are struggling, feeling all is lost, come unto Christ and commit yourself into His hands. We are all God's spirit children, and He loves each of us individually and is fully aware of who we are and what we can become.

I want to testify of living prophets on the earth in the latter days that receive revelation directly from God through the Holy Ghost. These prophets lead in a manner that God would have His children live and become more like Jesus Christ. I testify that it is not through teaching or learning of men but through the Holy Ghost that testifies to man eternal truths that will become pure knowledge if acted upon. I testify that through obedience, sincere repentance, and righteous living of all of God's commandments, He will provide a wonderful opportunity for each of His children to witness the eternal truths of the Plan of Salvation that has been prepared for all of us.

Lastly, I testify that a true conviction and recognition of the Holy Ghost of God's eternal plan will cause your personal inner existence to feel a calming feeling. Recognize the still, small voice that communicates to you, reassures you, enlightens you, encourages you, provides you comfort, and leads you in righteousness in all things, at all times, and in all places.

May the Lord's choicest blessing be with you always and forever!

About the Author

Brian Laine Heuett has devoted his life to teaching professionally as a professor of interpersonal communication and public speaking. He has been an independent consultant, traveling the United States and doing seminars teaching people about communication skills in the workplace and personal life. He has received several teaching awards, research awards, and Advisor of the Year awards in his profession. He has served in several leadership positions throughout his career. For example, he served as the faculty president-elect, faculty senate president, and director of the student success center, to mention a few. He received a bachelor's degree, master's degree, and PhD from Washington State University.

Brian has held several positions in the Church of Jesus Christ of Latter-day Saints. He has served as a bishop, high counselor, counselor in bishoprics, teacher in Sunday school courses, and seminary teacher for the Church Education System.

The author centers his message on the moral and spiritual aspects of good living, learning, and converting to the Lord, Jesus Christ. The text reflects on the conversion experience the author had to the Church of Jesus Christ of Latter-day Saints when he was yet a young man. He tells of his personal experiences he had via conversations with other people and through prayer and spiritual experiences he had. His desire is that the reader will find strength to overcome inadequacies, challenges, and trials and find success in turning their life over to God. "Into his hands I commit."